I0776078

Geographies of Memory/Landscapes of Ritual:

The Excavation of Forgotten Battlefield Presence

John G. Sabol

I.P.E. Research Center

Also by John Sabol...

Ghost Excavator (2007)

Ghost Culture (2007)

Gettysburg Unearthed (2007)

Battlefield Hauntscape (2008)

The Anthracite Coal Region (2008)

The Politics of Presence (2008)

Bodies of Substance, Fragments of Memory (2009)

Phantom Gettysburg (2009)

Digging Deep (2009)

The Re-Haunting(s) of Gettysburg (2010)

The Haunted Theatre (2011)

Ghost Culture Too (2012)

Beyond the Paranormal (2012)

Digging-Up Ghosts (2nd publishing, 2013)

Burnside Bridge (2013)

The Gettysburg Experience (2013)

The Absence Above, A Presence Below (2013)

The Production of Haunted Space (2013)

Centralia, Pennsylvania (2013)

The Ghost Excavation (2013)

The Good Death and the Civil War (2014)

Centralia: A Vision of Ruin (2014)

Altered States: Making the Extraordinary
Ordinary Again (2014)

Archaeology and Ghost Research: A Relational Entanglement (2014)

Performances in Haunted Space: An Afterlife in Ruin (2014)

Haunting Presences, Ruins, and Ghostly Entanglements (2015)

The Afterlife of Centralia: Presences in a Landscape of
Destruction (2015)

An Archaeology Without Borders: Performance Excavations in
Embedded/Entangled Fields (2016)

Ghost Hunt: Exploding the Myths/Exploring the Possibility (2016)

The Haunting of the Omni Bedford Springs Resort and Spa (2016)

The Haunting Presences of the Omni Bedford Springs (2017)

Victorian Ghosts of the Omni Bedford Springs:
Representation and Reveal (2017)

Walking the Ghostly Spaces of Bedford Springs:
The Movement of Presence (2017)

Geographies of Memory/Landscapes of Ritual:

The Excavation of Forgotten Battlefield Presence

Ghost Excavator Books, Inc. TM©

Bedford, Pennsylvania,
USA

Copyright 2017 by John G. Sabol and Ghost Excavation Books, Inc., Bedford, PA, USA. All rights reserved.

Front cover and back cover design by Mary Becker-Garofalo. Front cover, historical lithograph: *Battle of Antietam* (credit: unknown, public domain). Back cover photo: John Sabol, Antietam National Battlefield, Sharpsburg, Maryland, c. 2013 (credit: Mary Becker-Garofalo).

The right of John G. Sabol to be identified as the author of the text concepts has been asserted in accordance with section 77 and 78 of the Copyright, Design & Patent Act 1988.

Warning, the text herein is fully protected by U.S. Federal copyright laws. Federal copyright laws will be vigorously enforced and infringement will be prosecuted to the fullest extent of the law, which can include damages and lawyer's fees to be paid by the infringer of copyright. No part of this book may be reproduced or transmitted in any form or by any means including verbal, electronic or mechanical, and photocopying, recording or by any information storage and retrieval system without written permission from the publisher. For additional copyright information at cuicospirit@hotmail.com.

Photo credits: Historical archival photos; John Sabol; and, Mary Becker-Garofalo. All other photos, names, and original photos are used with permission and copyrighted by their respective owners.

Introduction

The geographic study of landscapes of violence is a field of increasing analysis. Most research has focused on how violence is remembered, a recognition that landscape serves to mark and materialize certain memories of that violence. Little research has centered on what has been forgotten that also materializes, and why these forms of materializations occur? Why do some landscapes of violence have an 'afterlife' presence that transcends time and contemporary representations portraying that violent past?

In this book, the unfolding of what is present in particular spaces of former violence is viewed through various geographical and social processes which include human, non-human, and haunting elements. What becomes present is the product, I propose, of historical, geographical, and ethnographic contingent affordances that allow particular presences of violence to remain embedded and attached to specific battlefield spaces.

A politics of memory and particular remembrances occur in specific geographies of violence, ones that highlight the fact that "what is commemorated is not synonymous with what has happened in the past" (Dwyer and Alderman 2008:167), or what may still remain. In such places, another past, another layer of memory, and an alternative form of remembrance has largely been forgotten. On battlefields, there is never simply one past, one memory, or one way to remember (Inwood 2009).

Preserved American Civil War battlefields are, for the most part, particular monuments to specific remembrances:

"transformed into sacred precincts, composed of immaculately tended lawns and forest edges marked with row upon row of stelae, obelisks, triumphal arches, megaliths, allegorical buildings, cannon, and sculptured figures" (Rainey 1997:67).

On these battlefields, "the memories evoked were highly select. There were no recollections of the brutality of total war..." (Ibid: 80). There was no remembering the sudden deaths, the mass unmarked graves, the incomplete rituals of rites of passage, or the haunting character that may still exist because of these social affordances.

Photo 1: The Monumentalization on the Gettysburg Battlefield

Photo 2: Monuments at Burnside Bridge, Antietam Battlefield (Sharpsburg, Maryland)

Today, in viewing these American Civil War battlefields, perceptions are lost as history is narrowly remembered. We have forgotten Marshall McLuhan's (1969) observations on the difficulty of separating image (the contemporary vista), meaning (what is missing), and message (the manicured battlefield). In most cases, the 'usual' scenes obstruct the unseen and un-sensed.

How might we reframe these battlefields? What about the unseen, the un-sensed, is it merely non-sense(d)? What other stories and social history might be told that still capture the haunting character of these battlefields? Those soldiers whose lives were obliterated on these battlefields, what forms of life remain, a life anchored away from the battlefield, and a time of still lingering Civil War?

Table of Contents

Photographs/Images

The Haunting Perspective

They share the weight of ritual. It keeps them bound to the battlefield.

"Survival is not possible if one approaches the environment, the social drama, with a fixed unchangeable POV – the witless repetitive response to the unperceived".

- Marshall McLuhan and Quentin Fiore

Ghosts, hauntings, and spectrality have increasingly become an area of research in various fields (Cameron 2008; Blanco and Peeren 2013; Lipman 2014; Lee 2017;

Hudson 2017). This includes heritage considerations (Herva 2014). Anna Karlstrom, an archaeologist at Uppsala University, has said that we should "take ghosts seriously as constitutive elements of heritage". Ladwig (2012) has said that "ghosts can be beings with desires…with biographies. They appear in specific ways, at certain places, at a certain time" (2012:23). The majority of this research, however, has been a representation for something other than 'dead humans' (cf. Blanco and Peeren 2010).

At death, a number of physical changes (and 'rites of passage') occur: a socio-cultural entity, with beliefs, experiences, and memories disappears. This is a universal aspect of human existence. A dead body, a cadaver emerges. But does anything of that socio-cultural entity remain after the emergence of the cadaver? Is that human completely transformed, as a final rite of passage, from flesh to bone to dust, and merely becomes part of a contemporary mortuary landscape or the archaeological record? Does some social character of a person survive? Does a liminal state, one between the flesh and the bone domains, exist? If so, how can we explore this materializing sense of presence, without consigning it to some supernatural agency or paranormal event? Are 'haunted' places/spaces merely 'haunted' by a perception (largely unfounded) of dead presence? Are 'haunted' locations merely a metaphor for something that is missing, lost, or forgotten, or are some 'haunted' places, and associated 'ghostly presences', real? Are we 'missing' that perspective?

In this turn to hauntings, the 'ghosts' of war have become especially dominant (Kwon 2006, 2008; Harjumaa 2008; Gustafsson 2009; Herva 2014, Arensen 2017, to name a few). Heonik Kwon (2008) sees ghosts and their haunting as expressions of socially-unprocessed deaths. Arensen (2017) has linked historical ghosts of the war dead, the massive disruption of the customary religious rites of Cambodian Buddhists, and the emotive materiality and affective presence of human bones scattered across the landscape.

In relation to this turn to 'war ghosts', rites of passage (especially the ritual of a 'good death') is prominent (see Sabol 2014a). This relationship between war and the 'good death' is part of the mortuary culture of many Asian societies with agrarian traditions. This tradition is a "house-centered morality of death" (Kwon 2006:12). Dying a 'good death' is "to die in the house and home" (Fox 1973:351). For a man, this involves dying "in his hut, lying on his bed, with his brothers and sons around him to hear his last words" (Middleton 1982:142).

The Good Death and Landscapes of Violence (Battlefields): Prelude to a Haunting?

When men die in battle, far from family and home, I propose, a haunting may occur. Such haunting experiences of ghostly presence are not considered out of the ordinary in Vietnam: "spirits are believed to influence and take part in the daily concerns of the living" (Gustafsson 2009:11). Contact with these entities are considered "extracultural" (Lambek 1981:29) because that contact does "not exist in a realm off-limits to humans" (Gustafsson 2009:13). These Vietnamese spirits are "angry ghosts", associated with the war dead who did not have the 'luxury' of being buried at home (cf. Malarney 2001). In Vietnam, families still make trips to search for remains of relatives who have died in combat far from home. Recent research has linked the archaeological record of battlefield sites and ghost/haunting phenomena (Herva 2014; Sabol 2014b; Sabol 2015)

In these examples, the context and explanation of a ghostly presence that haunts is relative to war, to not dying the 'good death'. This is because many remain buried in unknown locations far from home, and not being accorded the proper rituals as final acts of passage. Such ethnographic examples have, as Peter Metcalf (2001) suggests, "the power to put things in context, and that context is the explanation".

These 'ghosts of war' are not the same context, and thus explanation, as those described by Yael Navaro (2012) in her ethnography about the "affect that is discharged by a postwar environment" (2012:17), in the phantasmic entanglement of materialities in Northern Cyprus. For her, "the ghost is material…It exists in and through non-human objects…rather than standing as a representation of something or someone that disappeared or died…A ghost…is what is retained in material objects and the physical environment in the aftermath of the disappearance of the humans linked or associated with that thing or space" (Ibid: 17). Such objects and environments are shaped into Northern Cypriot social practices (Navaro 2012:17). This is only one part of the ecological (geographical) perspective of an ongoing haunting, its residual element. Consideration must also be given to the possibility of interactive elements, ones reinforced by this object residuality. These involve materializations as past sensory elements that continue to percolate in the present.

Still, the object represents the ghost. In this, it is analogous to contemporary 'ghost hunting', where various objects (such as light anomalies) and environmental deviations (such as drops in temperature) are indicative of a haunting. There is an overreaching optical character to contemporary paranormal thought: "the ghost looms in the cultural imagination first and foremost as things to be seen" (Leeder 2014:39). This has led to increasing use of 'ghost tech' devices and phone apps that increase this haunting optical character:

"The modern scientific and technological exploration of visions and optics (such as the proliferation of new optical devices) multiply and articulate the possibilities of the optical uncanny" (Gunning 2008:70).

The Archaeological Gaze:

A Sensing that Makes Sense

The basic assumption of this book is to comprehend landscapes of violence as an archaeological event. This can be perceived as an excavation into the social and cultural dimensions of a landscape of violence through the unearthing of layers of sensory memories. This is achieved in the form of a re-habitation of site through immersive performance practices (as 'excavation') in which one can associate and document particular movements, and sensory materializations, with specific topographical spaces. This links the physical experience of a landscape of violence to details of that experience, within a particular layer of embedded and attached memory.

This is to treat archaeological excavation as theater and layers of memory as scenes in this archaeological theater. This perspective is meant as a tool to unearth possible still attached past presence, and distinguish between embedded (residual) and attached (interactive) presences. This archaeological theater is not metaphoric, nor is it meant to re-construct or re-enact what was once there. It is not a form of 'edutainment' for a contemporary audience. It is meant to engage what still is and becomes present. It is a re-inhabitation of identity and situation, amid fields of memory.

Contemporary, context-specific performance practices afford, I propose, direct access to these layers of memory through sensory experience. Such an immersion continues an affective turn of the role of emotions, affordances, and affect as central research categories (cf. Budrewicz, et.al. 2014) in an entanglement of theater, performance, and archaeology (cf. Tilley 1989; Pearson and Shanks 2001; among others):

"An archaeological excavation is a theater of tasks...and hence a stage of interactions in a place often full of 'traces' of former interactions" (Victor Oliveira Jorge, 2007).

This layer of memory may be conceived of, I propose, as an unintentional form of "structured deposition" (Richards and Thomas 1984) which may form part of a layer of 'percolating' memory that still surfaces on battlefields today. It forms part of a battlefield's other archaeological record. Such layered deposits are examples of archaeological fieldwork in and of the present. They consist of surface assemblages (cf. Harrison 2011) of materializing past sensory elements.

At any site, there is no single past. There are multiple layers of potential, percolating pasts, such as these 'haunting' forms of 'structured deposits'. Their meaning, as that which remains, is always created within a particular socio-cultural context (cf. Barrett 1994). This affords them to become present, even those once thought dead and inactive. Such a becoming present of absent presence means that a site's archaeological record is not simply recovered, awaiting discovery. It must be creatively produced through particular performance practices, ones that afford materializations through effective remembrances of forgotten memories.

In every actuality of doing fieldwork (survey and/or excavation), many previously unexposed fragments (or 'structured deposits') of particular pasts are capable of being unearthed. What's more, what remains of an archaeological record is always open for argument, and potential exposure, many without additional economic considerations.

One thing in common in these haunting 'structured deposits' is the perception of 'ghostly phenomena'. But the manner in which that 'ghost of place' is sensed is always historically situated and culturally constituted (cf. Clarke 2013). In this book, my focus is the historical situation of mid-19th c. America. The culturally constituted layer of memory (as a 'structured deposit') is in a landscape of violence, specifically the American Civil War battlefield. Fieldwork involves a relation between the culture of war and the culture of death. Both were linked to particular rites of passage: 'seeing the elephant' (culture of war) and the Good Death (culture of death).

Making sense of this relationality in a 'structured deposit' involves a contemporary investigation as no mere 'digger', nor does it involve an "interpretation at the trowel's edge". Instead, one becomes a character within the memory layer of the 'structured deposit', experiencing (though not completely) what it meant to be in particular spaces on those battlefields, and the affordances of that immersion. It means to explore what was expected of a soldier in the social milieu in which they (not us) lived. It is to 'dig into' how we might have lived under the circumstances of that culture (and its relationality to war and death) in mid-Victorian society.

This immersion through the use of context-specific performance practices is not a version of an "archaeo-appeal" (Holtorf 2005) approach, an archaeology as response to a specific version of pop culture. It is not meant to create a particular vision of the past, or a form of 'ghost hunting'. It is a means to unearth an 'other' part of the archaeological record, one that is largely ignored or forgotten by archaeology.

Photo 3: An American Civil War Battlefield

~ *John G. Sabol* ~

Ghosts, Rites of Passage, and the American Civil War Battlefield

 According to Nancy Roberts (1992), "no history of war can compete with that of the American Civil War in terms of contributions to the American folkloric and literary tradition of ghost stories". But are these stories the reality of today's battlefield environment, as part of an ethno-historic context and explanation for perceived hauntings on these battlefields? Do they form a part of the archaeological record as a strata of memory defined as a "structured deposit", or are they merely made prominent by ghost hunters and reality TV programming through 'legend-tripping', misinterpretation and profitable forms of entertainment ('ghost tourism')?

The reality is that many American Civil War battlefields are huge, undocumented cemeteries, depositories of still large numbers (on some battlefields) of fallen, unknown soldiers who did not die a 'good death'. They remain (MIA), at locations of unknown interment, far from home and the family. Robert Blauner (1966), in the journal *Psychiatry,* demonstrated (using anthropological literature) that the early death of important members of the family result in ghost traditions. This tradition was reinforced, I propose, by the battlefield 'bad death' (unknown location; far from home; sudden death).

Sudden death, often common and widespread, was especially significant:

"Sudden death represented a profound threat to fundamental assumptions about the correct way to die, and its frequency on the battlefield comprised one of the most important ways that Civil War death departed from the 'ordinary death' of the prewar period" (Faust 2008:18).

American Civil War battlefields, time and again, broke societal norms by not providing opportune times, in many cases (such as instantaneous death), for the completion of the rite of passage of the Good Death. This occurred for the first time on a large and expansive scale.

Shaun Malarney (2002) has said that "Death on the battlefield was the quintessential bad death" (2002:179). Is this American Civil War battlefield entanglement (dying in battle far from home, and not accorded the rite of passage of a 'good death') one context-specific scenario that can ethnographically-explain why American Civil War battlefields are 'haunted'? The concept of 'home' itself was more than a powerful metaphor for these soldiers. It retained a powerful mnemonic affect throughout the war (1861-1865):

"Remembering home, dreaming of it...allowed men...to a certain extent to retain their pre-war identities" (Mitchell 2000:35).

The more established the ritual, the more likely it becomes attached to specific beliefs. This was an assumption "closely tied to the Victorian emphasis on the importance of home and domesticity" (Faust 2008:85). The rite of passage of the Good Death did affect behavior on the battlefield:

"Dying assumed clear preeminence over killing in the soldier's construction of his emotional and moral universe...They lived in a culture that offered many lessons in how life should end" (Faust 2008:6).

The "concept of the Good Death was central to mid-nineteenth-century America" (Ibid: 6), becoming "as much a part of respectable middle-class behavior in (the) North and South" (Faust 2008:7). It was a "concern shared by almost all Americans of every religious background" (2008:7). Such beliefs as the Good Death afforded how the ritual was to be correctly performed (and where), its social significance and purpose. But as Drew Faust (2008) states: "Civil War battlefields and hospitals could have provided the material for an exemplary text on how not to die" (2008:9). These battlefields became sites of haunting, I propose, because of broken, incomplete ritual time associated with the Good Death.

The change in this ritual culture, brought about by many battlefield deaths and unknown burial sites, resulted in a significant change in the associated ambiance of a Civil

War battlefield, even though "Civil War Americans worked to construct Good Deaths for themselves and their comrades amid the conditions that made dying-and living-so terrible" (Faust 2008:30).

Part of the pre-war Victorian identity was retained in this concept of a 'good death'. The American Civil War represented the transformation of a society, as a rite of passage, from one existing rhythm of mortuary culture (home; 'good death'; burial in the family plot; ritual, familiar mourning) to another (battlefield; far from home; MIA; 'bad death'). It was the passage for many soldiers from home to unknown that may have resulted in a haunting on some of these American Civil War battlefields.

Does a memory of 'home', as a domestic imagery, and the ritual of a 'good death', serve to afford a social technology of remembrance for those who died on these battlefields and who remain buried in unknown locations? Are American Civil War battlefields the final resting places for what Kwon (2008) has called a "displaced afterlife" in which the dead are "missing from one place and unknown in another place" (2008:85)? Are those dead, missing from home and whose locations of interment are unknown on the battlefield (and who have not been accorded the rite of passage of a 'good death' by surrogates) part of the ghost traditions mentioned by Roberts (1992)? Are these the perceptions frequently experienced and reported by visitors and ghost hunters on these battlefields? Is this context (an American Civil War battlefield containing a large number of unknown grave sites), and the ritual of the 'good death', prevalent in pre-Civil War America (as an ethno-historical reality), the reason (explanation) why these battlefields are haunted by presences from the past?

Image 4: The Good Death

In an article in *North American Archaeology* (Espenshade, et.al. 2002), the author's stress the "special nature of Civil War sites". They emphasize that the "battlefield dead were not comprehensively removed from the battlefield" (2002:41). They further suggest "that there is a real possibility that many Civil War sites contain human remains" (Ibid: 42). This adds to "both their research potential and sensitivity", complicated because "unlike typical cemeteries, there is often a lack of formal, carefully aligned grave features". Are these battlefield realities more than an archaeological concern for the recovery of remains? Is there still a humanitarian concern for locating and identifying these remains, and for their transport back to 'home' sites? Is that part of this archaeological 'sensitivity'? Finally, what about completion of the rite of passage of the Good Death? Is that also a part of archaeological 'research potential'?

The idea of returning the dead to be buried at home has been a part of United States policy since the American Civil War. But does the pre-war concept of 'home', the rite of the 'good death', have other social implications and affects? Does it afford lingering presences to still remain today? Do these presences have conscious memories, ones still attached to these battlefields? If so, do we have an obligation to finalize the rite of passage for these potential 'haunting presences' by retrieving their remains and returning them 'home' to their place of residence?

American Civil War battles broke societal norms by not providing opportune times, in many cases, for completing (for the first prolonged time) the societal tradition of the Good Death ritual. It re-shaped behavior and presence on these battlefields. It produced haunting phenomena, affording ghostly attachments. Death, especially an instantaneous one, and burial in unknown locations, put a high emotional stress on the cognitive framework of deep-seated cultural ideals, like the Good Death ritual.

This re-structured a societal-base rite of passage eliminating, in many instances, an expediency of moral action within a still widely-held tradition of death rituals. Such a tradition still existed, in a complex and bound relationship, at the time of the outbreak of the American Civil War. The American Civil War battlefield afforded for the first time a potential American 'army of ghosts', by the exclusion, in many cases, the rite of passage of the Good Death.

The Battlefield as Ritual Theater: Haunting Implications

Combat is a socio-cultural act, a rite of passage. During the American Civil War, it was "seeing the elephant". It is a ritual performed with the rules of the culture of war regarding space (the so-called K.O.C.O.A. configuration) and behavior (Inherent Military Probability (I.M.P.) or how the soldier would have performed in these K.O.C.O.A. spaces). The K.O.C.O.A., which stands for key area, observation area, cover and concealment area, obstacle area, and avenue of approach, is part of METT-T

("Mission, Enemy, Terrain, Troops-Time"), involved in the planning of tactical operations. It was the military terrain strategy, for specific acts of I.M.P. behavior, used during the American Civil War.

K.O.C.O.A. represents the 'stage' of combat performance. Each K.O.C.O.A. space is a different scene, consisting of particular set pieces, requiring particular acts, using specific 'props'. One of these 'props' was the bugle. During the American Civil War, there were 57 different bugle calls (for infantry movements). These bugle calls (together with officer commands and drum beats) controlled battlefield behaviors. In the K.O.C.O.A. spaces, they served as the "trowel" in "excavating" these spaces during performance-enacting scenarios that were used as social affordances to 'unearth' past presence in our field investigations on these battlefields (see below).

K.O.C.O.A. is culturally relative. It does not represent 'best military practice' but rather the military practices of the period being analyzed: how individual dispositions filtered a conception and perception of the terrain (or 'habitus'). Keegan (1993) stated that culture has a profound impact on how battles are approached: as a myriad entanglement of experience, ideology, norms, and traditions, each context-specific to a time and space (cf. 1993:12). This 'grammar' of conflict on a battlefield is important. It determined the difference between what one should do and what occurred on the battlefield.

During the American Civil War, this 'grammatical' entanglement also involved the Good Death ritual. It is this difference between what one should do, and what one did (based on circumstances) regarding the Good Death rite of passage that produced the liminality of American Civil War battlefields, a haunted landscape. It is the difference between performing a completed rite of passage (a Good Death) as a ''surrogate' family member, and not being able to do so, due to the manner of death (obliteration) or the time of death. This opens-up the execution of a rite of passage for completion by a future 'surrogate family member', even one remote in time, but not in behavior (see battlefield 'excavation' below).

These 'rules' of combat and battlefield terrain analysis were implemented (and reinforced) by pre-battle drills of movement, augmented by 'soundmarks' (drums, bugle calls, and officer commands). During the American Civil War, there were 15 basic drum-beat signals and 57 bugle calls to learn. Artillery units and cavalry had their own bugle calls, so an infantryman had to be able to distinguish a message intended for him, and one designed for an entirely different branch of military service.

If places are selected and used because they contain interaction-specific capabilities (such as those identified in a K.O.C.O.A. configuration) for certain behavioral acts (such as specific I.M.P. behaviors), then a battlefield represents specific performance practices performed there and experienced, those that remained in memory during the rite of 'seeing the elephant', and used as mnemonic devices on other battlefields. Do these practices survive as ghostly, materialization phenomena? Today, do embedded battlefield sounds, imprinted onto the environment, reinforce 'attached' presences who may remain embedded in unknown graves on the battlefield, and who await the termination of the rite of passage of the Good Death?

Like a rite of passage, there are separate stages to combat in the American Civil War culture of war:

- Separation: pre-battle drilling;
- Liminality: the battle itself; and
- Transformation: the survival of 'seeing the elephant' or death.

In this 'rite', if the former was achieved, personal memories of that transformation would continue to 'haunt' the living the rest of their lives. If death occurred, without the proper rituals of a 'good death' (performed by surrogates, such as fellow soldiers or the medical corps), the uncompleted ritual process would, I propose, still haunt the dead. A battlefield haunting may be the effect of this 'bad death'.

Civil War battlefields today are sites of this collective memory. The memorials, guided tours, and re-enactments represent contemporary overt 'sights' of remembrance that something historical has occurred there. Through these materializations, this becomes a contemporary viewers (an 'outsider' etic perspective) to what is selected as remembrance. However, for those dead that may remain embedded and 'lost' on the battlefield (far from 'home'), and still 'attached' to the concept of a 'good death' (an 'insider' emic perspective), the hauntings that are reported on these battlefields may be a 'sensual' sign of a different form of remembrance, a memory forgotten by most visitors to the battlefields today.

For both the living visitor, and the 'attached' dead, the ritual of battle, I propose, "frequently involve(s) a practical remembering effected through the experience and manifestation of symbolic material items" (Barth 1987:75). For the living, it is monumentalization and re-enactment. For the dead, still 'missing in action', it is still the ritual of the 'good death'. The incomplete ritual of the 'good death', as a particular rite of passage through the passage of 'seeing the elephant', remains unfulfilled. This affected an attachment, I propose, to these battlefields so powerful that, in some cases, lead to a haunting. The battlefield remains a 'liminal' space for those soldiers that are still in a 'liminal' state of this dual ritual process.

The increased popularity and importance of Spiritualism during and after the American Civil War was a direct result, I propose, of this continuing liminal state between both the living, who sought closure, and the battlefield dead, those who remained 'lost' on the battlefield in unknown grave sites. The problem with Spiritualism at this time was not so much an attempt at closure, as it was the location. A séance in the home was not the proper space for completing this rite of passage *after* death (though many families were not aware of the status of their loved ones), like it was *before* death. The battlefield, I propose, was the affording space for this ritual enactment, and still is.

Note:

I know of no reports of séances performed on Civil War battlefields during or immediately following the end of the American Civil War. At Gettysburg, the site of a horrific and deadly three day battle, there are no reports of séances there, and this includes the town (during and immediately following the Civil War).

~ John G. Sabol ~

The Excavation of Battlefield Hauntings: Introduction

How do we investigate the possibility of American Civil War battlefield hauntings? If the battlefield is the proper space for an alternative ritual performance of the rite of passage of the Good Death, how can we make closure for those who may remain in unmarked locations on the battlefield? The investigation of possible American Civil War battlefield hauntings must be linked in ethnographic terms. As David Orr (1994) suggests, a linkage must be made "to the anthropological values of the battle's participants" (1994:33). The haunting, if it exists, must reveal traces of both the American Civil War's culture of war (an entanglement between K.O.C.O.A. spaces and materializations of I.M.P. behaviors) and the culture of the 'good death'. These traces must be related to the social realities of battlefield combat during the American Civil War.

A simple phenomenological walk and instrument survey of the battlefield is problematic. We cannot re-create the sensory environment, the thunderous, deafening, and deadly battlefield soundscape, and the visual impairment from tremendous rifle and artillery fire; nor can we model the emotional and psychological impact that triggered the experience of 'seeing the elephant'. But we can complete the post-battle social behavior of Civil War-era family searches. We can simulate and enact those rites of the Good Death as surrogate family members in specific K.O.C.O.A. spaces. These would be located where concentrated, horrific, and rapid death would have occurred during battle, based on the historical record.

The American Civil War battlefield was not perceived, experienced, or remembered as a landscape of combat. It became a 'soundscape'. 'Seeing' the elephant' was achieved through 'soundmark' cues. The experience of battle assaulted a soldier's sensorium, especially its sounds of destruction and death. The pre-battle drills did not prepare the soldiers for battle. It afforded merely a visual guide, a baseline, which disappeared through intensive fire power. Sight was at a premium. It was surprising (to these soldiers) how little they could actually see. At the first major battle, Bull Run (or Manassas Junction):

"When the Rhode Islanders lay down – and they often did – they found that all they could make out was the red Virginia soil beneath them…But mostly their foe was invisible...factor reducing visibility was the smoke bellowing from all the muskets and cannon...No breezes wafted the smoke away from the battlefield, so it hung like a London fog between the two sides..." (Detzer 2004:256-257).

This reduction of visibility become a 'commonality of experience' on most American Civil War battlefields, as was the ensuing sounds of war:

"the gasping, the panting, the grunting of men...the ripping open of cartridges, the rattle of ramrods plunging into musket barrels, the clink of canteens against metal, the squealing wheels of artillery vehicles, the drum signals, the shouting and swearing" (Ibid: 257).

For the common American Civil War soldier in battle, the universe shrank. It compressed to specific fields of social behavior and experience, the I.M.P that formed a context for how to engage (based principally on auditory 'cues') the enemy. Today, some of these auditory cues, without visual presence and reminiscent of what happened on the battlefield, still continue to percolate as embedded environmental residuals, imprinted upon the environment. We have recorded many of these residual battlefield sounds on various American Civil War battlefields.

The American Civil War's culture of war was framed by this battlefield soundscape. Anthropologist Alexander Lesser (1961) uses the term "social field" to describe the "web-like connections" between individuals and their social groups and, I propose, these environmental residuals that stretch across time and space.

A particular type of haunting, a social (battlefield) haunting, emerged. It is the outcome, I propose, of environmental scaffolding (recurring residual manifestations) that affords particular memories to be recalled by any attached presences who may remain on the battlefield. These 'ghost soldiers', as interactive presences, may represent 'afterlife' mental processes, as a form of 'extended mind' (cf. Clark and Chalmers 1998). These mental processes are:

- <u>Extended:</u> they include wider bodily processes that afford (and are accompanied by) context-specific sensory elements;
- <u>Embedded:</u> they function only in relation to a certain environment (that is environmentally-scaffolded) outside the brain;
- <u>Enacted:</u> they involve how the entity ('ghost soldier') acts on the world, and the way the world acts back (through recurring residuals); and

- <u>Extended:</u> they extend out into the entity's immediate environment (the battlefield).

Together, they form, I propose, an assemblage of an interactive 'ghost battle', consisting of those who remains attached to a particular battlefield space (K.O.C.O.A.). The haunting illustrates how an assemblage of things (environmental auditory manifestations) can maintain historical identity of a particular layer of communal agency. Particular 'identities', in the form of attached Civil War soldiers, are still maintained there, not through post-battle ritualization that narrate history (monuments; historical markers) or re-created, in a superficial, non-context-specific way (re-enactment), but through continuing (and percolating) 'soundmark' environmental residuals, and attached presences, as a particular way of (still) knowing a place (an 'acoustemology' – Feld 1996). This serves as a contemporary means of conceptualizing a social haunting through identity. Identity is thus an emergent property of affording assemblages (non-human and human) which includes place (K.O.C.O.A.), performance (I.M.P. behaviors), and 'ritualistic' objects (drums, bugles) as issues of experience, memory, affordance, and affect.

If a Civil War battlefield is a contemporary mortuary landscape of many unknown soldiers, are the hauntings that are perceived there the reinforcements of that character? A search for these dead to reconnect to the living (to complete the rite of passage of the 'good death'), then, can be understood as an important component in a contemporary (and haunting) remembrance for these unknown dead. The haunting becomes a production (a 'reoccupation') of a battlefield space which entangles a still incomplete ritual act tied to members of a given cultural tradition who are still embedded in a liminal state, betwixt and between death and their 'afterlife'.

Anthropologist Tim Ingold (2008) writes this about the environment: It "comprises not the surroundings of the organism, but a zone of entanglement" (2008:1797). A conclusion to consider about the possibility of American Civil War battlefield 'haunting' phenomena is that this potential zone of 'entanglement' necessitates a different strategy of investigative immersion. The Civil War battlefield, besides its historical significance, may also represent a temporal entanglement between present and past, absence and presence, and the living and the dead which require context-specific performance practices to ascertain whether this entanglement still exists in contemporary reality.

Of great importance, is the empathetic connection of such performance practices to memory and ritual, a sort of syncretism which suggests a continuing obligation between people and the "ghosts" of place, as it relates to time, social behavior, memory, remembrance, and ritual in specific battlefield spaces. It means we have to un-bound our concept of a tranquil, historically dormant place in order to unbind potential embedded presences that may still remain bound to certain ritual acts. This is not 'ghost hunting'. It is completing a past rite of passage for soldiers that are still 'MIA'. It shows how battlefields may still be entangled to past (uncompleted) acts that require action, how its spaces continue to be sites of a still needed ritualization of remembrance that has been forgotten or ignored today.

A Civil War battlefield remains active and connected to such rituals and memory, as well as an attachment to the American Civil War culture of war. This connection is not fully realized and exhibited through historical or contemporary 'monument building', historical markers, museum displays, and re-enactments or 'living history' presentations. The manifestation of perceived and reported ghostly presences, involving multiple sensorial modalities (haptic, acoustic, olfactory, visual), still appears to be occurring on these battlefields. There are still unknown 'restless' dead on these battlefields. These battlefield ghosts, I propose, are inseparable from their particular social attitudes to death (the 'good death'), as well as still entangled to specific historical circumstances of their death (on a battlefield far from home and family). The battlefield remains a theater of war for these attached presences.

The rituals associated with the culture of war and the rite of passage of the 'good death' emplace individuals in various positions of separation (on battlefields far from home), liminality ("seeing the elephant"), and re-incorporation/transformation (survive and go 'home'; die, but receive the 'good death' ritual via surrogates; die, with the ritual of the 'good death' still incomplete, and remain embedded on the battlefield, attached to the ritual, and 'haunting' the present). When a place, such as a battlefield, is ritually structured with distinct stages of separation, liminality, and transformation, its character becomes discontinuous (cf. Thorn 2013). This 'discontinuity', I propose, becomes a 'social haunting' that continues today on these battlefields, thus altering the concept of a linear time frame.

Time, on a landscape of violence (such as a battlefield) is not simply a collection of fragmented remains of artifacts or fossilized trace scenes depicted on historical markers. It is not always a peaceful, contemporary physical environment, either. Nor is it the battle's K.O.C.O.A. spaces still present among scattered historical monuments. Time is a continuous haunting process, incorporating the interactions of multiple temporalities and affording effects. Each has different resonant qualities, allowing hauntings to maintain presence and materialize. Such materializations reveal an 'other' more complex historical reality: assembling and assembled elements, alternative (though not 'fringe' or 'paranormal') historical narratives, 'ghost stories', and forms of life still present. It is to their 'excavation' that I now turn.

The 'Excavation' of Battlefield Hauntings; Methodology

The question remains: how do we investigate this possibility? Fieldwork, one grounded in a phenomenological interpretative tradition, as "event ethnography", may be one means. Such a perspective offers new possibilities for sensing, thinking, acting, and interpreting continuing forms of (past) life in the present. Such "an extension of perceiving" (Gibson 1986:258) changes the way we look at the world and these landscapes of violence. This can aid in the recognition of possible previously unnoticed entanglements between different phenomena and those cultural processes still in need of completion.

An experiential approach requires the investigator to take a specific participatory role in the social world of these possibly still active battlefields. In such a role, one must "become one's own informant" (Favret-Saada 1980:22). It is an ethnographic stance where participation, perception, and experience become active agents of knowing a place. By putting oneself within, inhabiting a sense of a world, as it was sensed, is to become "passionately interested in the coproduction of ethnographic knowledge" (Tedlock 1991:82). This gives no precedent to an outsider, etic perspective.

This may be achieved by what has been termed "ghost ethnography" (Armstrong 2010). This is a "reflection in ethnographic practice and presents linkages (with) spatial, ideological, and material resonance in the…spaces of cultural production" (2010:248). On an American Civil War battlefield, this linkage would involve K.O.C.O.A. (spatial), the Good Death rite of passage (ideological), and acoustical producers (people and material objects) that afford 'soundmarks' on a battlefield that was more a soundscape than a landscape.

Note:

The K.O.C.O.A. was used as a desk-based assessment to construct, in advance of field 'excavation', the terrain of a particular American Civil War battlefield to be used in the investigation. Burnside Bridge, on the Antietam battlefield in Maryland, the site of the deadliest single day of combat in American History (September 16, 1862) was chosen. This location was selected because much of the original K.O.C.O.A. terrain is still intact. The key area (the bridge), though modified and recently re-constructed, is still in place. The observation area (the 'Georgia Overlook'), cover and concealed areas (such as the one near the present 11th Connecticut Monument), the obstacles (the stone wall; Antietam Creek; wooden fences), and the avenue of approach (Rohrbach Farm Road) are all still in place. Burnside Bridge also has minimal 'monumentalization' (unlike places such as Gettysburg) which might 'confuse' any attached presences who may still remain there.

Photo 5: The "Key Area"

Photo 6: The "Observation Area"

Photo 7: The "Cover and Concealed Area"

Photo 8: The "Obstacle Area"

Photo 9: The "Avenue of Approach"

The 'ghost ethnography' is also a means to emotionally and empathetically pass from one finite field of experience and meaning to another. This becomes a transduction, a transformation and integration, as a final step in a rite of passage. It can entangle another reality and temporality and, at the same time, can disentangle past presences from remaining attached to the battlefield. It can unlock a layer of memory to a particular presence, situation, and time.

How can we do this on a Civil War battlefield when we cannot experience "seeing the elephant"? One way is to relate objects with time, since "objects anchor time" (Tuan 1977:123). The manifestation of presence through a resonance to a particular layer of memory, using object cues, may be created by entangling the living with the embedded battlefield dead through social "technologies of remembrance" (Johnson and Schneider 2013).

Herva (2014) states that "things become alive-or their agency activated-when people come to interact in whatever form with wartime sites and things" (2014:308). Such active presence is conceived "in terms of relational ontology and epistemology" and involves presences which haunt the present "not just metaphorically but also in a more literal sense" (Ibid: 308).

In the context of a Civil War battlefield, these ethnographic linkages (in a "ghost ethnography") can come about through participatory practices of I.M.P. behaviors using 'soundmark cues' onto a 'remembered' soundscape setting. These "technologies of remembrance" were produced by specific material objects (drums, bugles, weaponry) that resulted in a battlefield sensorium, or acoustemology (Feld 1996). This produced a distinct way of knowing a place, one that entangles a continuing relation, through percolating environmental (residual) scaffolding, present and past. These residuals form a medium that affords a continuing haunting presence. It is a 'communication' from a living environment (of both past and present). These residuals become the 'voices' of memory, as the battlefield, even today, is foremost a 'listening' environment. It consists of histories of listening that occurred during and long after the battle was fought. Such entanglements can produce a continuity of time in specific spaces through rituality (Gheorghiu 2013), and the generation of a ritual time (cf. Bloch 1977), as a rite of passage (VanGennep 1960).

Feld (1996) pioneered field methodologies that connect phenomenological and environmental emplacements of soundings and listening into ethnographic research as a way of knowing a place (what is knowable and how it becomes known). In fieldwork on battlefields, the sounding of (as culturally-cued affordances) and recordings become a way of knowing the battlefield's haunting embedded and attached presences. Sound is viewed as "situational" (Haraway 1988) among "related subjects" (Bird-David 1999), such as soldiers on a battlefield who sense (and know) the place as a soundscape rather than a landscape. Sounds on the battlefield were the 'eyes' that both created (and prevented) flow and movement through the K.O.C.O.A. spaces.

Sound becomes a manifestation that informs experience, a basic element of how we frame knowledge. It centralizes 'situated' listening when engaging particular spatial and temporal parameters, such as the K.O.C.O.A. spaces on an American Civil War battlefield. Such situational and relational elements allow contemporary investigators to prioritize a particular history of sound experience, and what this afforded the soldier in battle. Subsequently, any manifesting residual sounds would produce a resonating mode of acoustic attending (a sonic affordance) that recalls memory. The battlefield becomes a 'marked' place, made by the soldiers who fought and died there. This 'marking' was achieved through performance practices guided by 'soundmarks'. These I.M.P. practices were performed in and, I propose, through time. An American Civil War battlefield became a resonant site of military and cultural memory and identity construction.

Also, the Civil War battlefield was a "hi-fi soundscape" (Schafer 1977). This is "one possessing a favorable signal to noise ratio" (Ibid: 43). A battlefield emphasized sounds intended for "audition" (Skinner 2005). Audition is "socially embedded in practice and historically emergent in process". The use of soundmarks (such as drums, bugle calls, and officer commands), used on American Civil War battlefields, are forms of 'audition'. Their acoustical manifestations in particular K.O.C.O.A. spaces emphasized this 'audition' over acoustic distortion ('noise', such as natural sounds). They became meaningful on the battlefield in the form of I.M.P. behaviors in specific K.O.C.O.A. spaces. We can use such resonance in a similar way in 'excavating' these K.O.C.O.A. spaces.

The use of bugle and drums, as 'excavation' tools, produce context-specific 'soundmarks' as a way "to develop satisfactory accounts of how some objects come to hold specific meanings for different people, and how these meanings are sometimes promoted to semiotic ideologies" (Preucel 2016:5). These 'sound' tools represent an effective means to reinhabit a battlefield as an 'excavation'. The use of sounds becomes an emotional extension, affecting memory across and between spaces and time. The bugle and drum become 'ritual objects' that revive memory.

This entanglement between objects, layers of memory, and ritual practices provide a meaningful co-habitation of battlefield space, one that does not significantly alter perception and remembrance over time. This relational resonance offers the possibility of continuing, and finally terminating, the rite of passage of the Good Death through the unearthing of emotions and experiences tied to a new process of action. This is the repeated process of using and occupying a space of ritualistic liminality (the battlefield). Context-specific performance practices, as the process of 'excavation' serves as a 'bridge' that crosses from past to present. The use of objects, as sensorial elements, have a positional value in entangling temporalities, serving in the capacity of symbolic practices of ritualistic design.

In our investigations on the Antietam battlefield, in Maryland (USA), and specifically at Burnside Bridge on that battlefield, we performed context-specific scenarios that mimicked I.M.P. behaviors in various battlefield spaces of the K.O.C.O.A. configuration (see Sabol 2014a; 2015). We used specific 'soundmarks' in each of these spaces to try to identify still embedded behaviors (as 'ghostly presences') associated with the culture of war (I.M.P. behaviors). As Steven Feld (1994) has stated:

"Each hearing, like human social interaction generally, has...a biography and a history, and these may be more or less important to the particular hearing in question at a specific time" (1994:89).

Using these contextual soundmarks (specifically particular bugle calls), linked to our re-creating (as a form of 'reinhabiting' the battlefield landscape) scenarios based on the historical record in specific K.O.C.O.A. spaces, we hoped to re-entangle these soundmarks/scenarios to manifestations of context-specific auditory phenomena of I.M.P. behaviors. Through this process of 're-inhabiting' the battlefield soundscape, we hoped to establish ourselves as 'insiders' ('emically-placed') through a remembrance of the soldier's cultural memory and our identity construction as Civil War soldiers. If memory and identity were restored (see results below and at www.ghostexcavation.com "Antietam"), we would then move on to identify ourselves as 'family' and perform the final stage of the rite of passage of the 'good death', resulting in the transformation and transition to another state of being, with past presences ('ghost soldiers') no longer attached to particular K.O.C.O.A. spaces.

Note:

By identifying K.O.C.O.A. spaces of potential attached presences, we hoped to locate zones where actual physical remains of soldiers were still buried. We hoped to supplement the 'excavation' with the use of ground penetrating radar to locate possible disturbances which might be indicative of burials. At the time of this writing, the application of ground penetrating radar has not been used.

Ghost Ethnography as Ethno-archaeological 'Excavation'

The task of our fieldwork was to 'excavate' the traces of past lives on the battlefield as a part of culture (the culture of war). It centered on remains that may have been inscribed onto the materiality of particular K.O.C.O.A. spaces by still attached presences. These presences consist of those soldiers who did not receive a completed rite of passage of the Good Death. The 'excavation', using specific performance scenarios ('simming' particular I.M.P. behaviors), and context-specific to specific K.O.C.O.A. spaces, are used to animate, rather than mimic, past behaviors and experiences (cf. Vannini 2015:318), thus stimulating the memory of those attached presences.

The 'excavation' as "ghost ethnography" is a form of non-representational ethnography, an "alternative approach that actively incorporates the experiential, affective, and inter-material aspects of (a haunted) space" (Hayward 2012:449). It is a form of "re-inhabiting" the battlefield through animation, not re-enactment. This permits investigators, as participants, to create a 'theater' of operating I.M.P. practices, allowing them to enter the emotions and experiences of another world and time (cf. Atkinson 1989:15). It can transform absence on a battlefield into another state of materializing being (the presence of 'ghosts').

The K.O.C.O.A. configuration, as a baseline for this excavation, follows the concept of a form of "inhabitation" (Barrett 2000). This involves the way contemporary investigators can establish <u>their</u> presence at a past site of occupation without the entanglement of the socio-political conditions and horrific conditions and dangers of a battlefield landscape. This establishes a structured field of remembrance, linked to dimensions of time (the American Civil War) and space (specific K.O.C.O.A. parameters). These are mapped, and performance practices of specific I.M.P. behaviors are enacted in alignment with specific situations, as stratigraphic units of memory. The goal is to link contemporary sensual experiences to possible emotional attachments relative to a still liminal state of an incomplete rite of passage of the Good Death. The contemporary in-habitation, as re-habitation of the battlefield landscape, is a means to complete the last stage of the rite of passage of the Good Death, through the use of investigators as 'surrogate family'.

In a performance 'excavation', we attempt to make contact, as the first step, to locate embedded presences through the use of context-specific material culture. On an American Civil War battlefield, that material culture is based on objects that are relative to 'soundmarks' (bugles, drums). The use of these objects involves a comparability of context and sensuality as relational resonance. It considers how an archaeological approach can "combine the material (artifacts) and immaterial (investigators using military commands) in cultural performances to achieve specific semiotic effects" (Preucel 2016:6). This suggests that "certain meanings composed of sign bundles-ways of handling and talking about particularly valued signs-can be given preeminent status and, by virtue of this, exert social agency" (Ibid: 6).

If materializing elements are recorded, we continue interaction through the execution of reiterative responses as I.M.P. behaviors until manifestations cease. We then attempt to be identified as 'surrogate family', either in search of lost love ones on the battlefield or as fellow soldiers on the battlefield, who can complete the rite of passage of a Good Death. In this two-step excavating process, artefacts (bugles, drums) both carry meaning and secondary agency, effectively enabling an active role in the construction of cultural identity (cf. Kristiansen 2011:202) to become established. The 'excavation' itself is a particular use of personhood. The investigators are themselves 'acting' as instruments of research by participating through their use of context-specific artefacts, those that can create meaningful 'soundmarks' onto a contemporary battlefield setting. The performance practices thus afford remembrance: the memory of what happened there, and what remains to be completed.

 A few of the scenarios that were enacted at Burnside Bridge included:

- A 'roll-call' of the 11th Connecticut in a cover and concealed area, initiated by a specific bugle call to assemble the men;
- An order to 'charge' up the Rohrbach Farm Road (as an 'avenue of approach') toward the bridge (as the 'key area'), initiated by another bugle call and drum roll; and
- An historical narrative (use of actual historical narrative of commanding officer speech to the 51st New York and 51st Pennsylvania) near the bridge to finalize the assault (by the same) to cross it and move toward the Confederate positions.

These performance practices, using context-specific I.M.P. behaviors, were meant to afford assembly for combat, a charge toward the key area as combat ('seeing the elephant'), and, for many, death on the battlefield at and near Burnside Bridge (the 'key area'). It is in the last K.O.C.O.A. space that many died without being accorded the rite of passage of the Good Death.

In each scenario, we recorded and documented various context-specific auditory 'responses' (materializing and context-specific to our performances). During the 'roll-call', we had 'voices' acknowledge the mention of *their* names. The 'role call' was enacted at the 11th Connecticut Monument (a cover and conceal area). The names used were the 39 soldiers who were killed during the 1st assault toward the key area (Burnside Bridge). During the simulated charge, we recorded the sounds of combat on the Rohrbach Farm Road (the avenue of approach for many of the Union assaults). During the final assault, we recorded the 'discharge' of rifle fire at the bridge (see www.ghostexcavation.com ("Antietam")) to listen to these recordings.

Photo 10: The Scenario at the 11th Connecticut Monument

Photo 11: The Scenario at the 11th Connecticut Monument

Subsequently, we performed context-specific scenarios relative to the concept of the 'good death'. These were enacted at or near the Key Area (Burnside Bridge) where many Union soldiers died. We had female investigators, dressed in mid-19th c. clothing, search for lost 'loved ones' on the battlefield at or near the bridge and the nearby stone wall. The names and associations of these 'surrogate' family members were identified through a search of records from the 1860 census. Such practices of family searches on the battlefield were common during the American Civil War:

"Desperate families, both North and South, traveled by the hundreds to battlefields to search in person for missing kin" (Faust 2008:127).

Photo 12: The 'Search' Scenario

Photo 13: The Search Scenario

During the American Civil war, a "soldiers' personal possessions often took on the character of *memento mori,* relics that retained and represented something of the spirit of the departed" (Faust 2008:29). However, these relics did not replace the search as a cultural response to those missing in battle. Dying a Good Death, by performing a complete rite of passage, still took precedence.

A Civil War battlefield remembrance, as an attempt to locate and recover those missing and lost in battle, stands in stark contrast to what occurred after World War I in England. The enormous number of missing, together with the British decision not to repatriate the dead (Winter 1995:27) resulted in a distancing process between those who remembered and those who were remembered, such that "the memory of the body (was) replaced by the memory of the object" (Stewart 1994:33).

This took the form of trench art souvenirs (Lloyd 1994:131). It created a symbolic landscape of remembrance (Winter 1995), rather than a search and recovery operation. The souvenirs enabled the living "to carry home a tangible link with the memory…of the dead" (Lloyd 1994:185). This focused on living memory, not the memory of possible embedded battlefield dead. Did this create a different and reduced form/frequency of Battlefield hauntings on the Western Front? Perhaps.

Some of the 'surrogate' scenarios, regarding the Good Death rite of passage that we enacted at or near Burnside Bridge were the following:

- Female investigators, portraying women in the 'household' of Lt. Colonel William Holmes, 2nd Georgia, and using the names recorded on the 1860 census as living in his household in Georgia, performed a search for him on the battlefield. Holmes is still MIA, and his gravesite in Georgia is empty; and

- Another female investigator, portraying a 'relative' of Pvt. John Thompson, 51st New York, who died during the final assault, walked with a lantern along the stone wall parallel to Antietam Creek, asking what happened to him on the battlefield. In the same location, there is a photograph, taken mere days after the battle. In the photo, there are five graves, each with a marker. One of those graves was that of Pvt. John Thompson, who later was interred in the Civil War cemetery in nearby Sharpsburg, Maryland.

In the case of Lt. Colonel Holmes, we got numerous 'responses' saying where 'he' is located. He also 'told' us he wanted to go 'home'. Regarding Pvt. John Thompson, we got an audio response that sounded like cannonfire, suggesting to us that this is what happened to him. (go to www.ghostexcavation.com ("Antietam") to hear these recordings).

These semiotic connections, verified through the identification of homologous context-specific audio recordings (EVP or Ethnographies of Communication (EOC)), reveal symbolic conventions, such as soldier identity and response to performance practices, simulating context-specific I.M.P. behaviors. They form what Pauketat (2001) calls a "genealogy of practices" within particular K.O.C.O.A. spaces. This behavioral focus on a relationality between still attached presences ('extended minds'), embedded environmental residuals, ritualistic practices, memory, and spaces indicate, I propose, physical and social affordances that continue across time, stimulating a remembrance of battle <u>and a continuing belief in the rite of passage of the Good Death,</u> manifesting as various sensory signatures at Burnside Bridge.

Summary

An American Civil War battlefield haunting was viewed as a particular form of landscape inscription, one directly related to a lack of cultural intervention on the part of the living, resulting in a 'bad death'. The haunting manifestations on a Civil War battlefield become what Kern (1983) calls a "cultural artifact". This is a particular sensorial layer of memory, anchored in time and space, attached to particular cultural constructions. But there is more. Presences, associated with the haunting, are forms of life that remain in a liminal state of existence.

This layer of memory forms a 'ghost culture', assembled as an 'afterlife' world of remains that include a relation between things (stone, trees, water, fences) and presences. They form a baseline for 'imprinting' a continuing identity as an American Civil War battlefield and soldiers onto the physical environment of the contemporary environment at Burnside Bridge, Antietam Battlefield.

For too long, a haunting agency has been assigned primarily to the activities, perceptions, beliefs, and misinterpretations of humans alone. In this perspective, it is the 'ghost' (as a 'dead human') who manifests because of some unresolved issue; or, it is the contemporary human who, because of some psychological or physical issue, perceives what they believe to be a haunting, or misinterprets/misunderstands 'normal' physical (environmental) processes at work.

Here, a haunting is constructed as the product of a hybrid network which includes humans (both past and present), things, the natural environment, and cultural beliefs and rituals. The non-human elements, as affecting objects and physical processes do not merely stand for, symbolize, or represent a haunting. A haunting begins, endures, and manifests through a series of affordances, both environmental and socio-cultural:

- Material fragments of presence, what remains archaeologically after an event, or is brought to a site as memorialization or context-specific material culture;
- Physical elements, indigenous to a place, such as water, wind, light, and sound that can embed presence; and
- Certain experiences and memories of place that result in post-mortem attachments.

This becomes the assemblage, relationally connected that haunts a place or landscape. This assemblage consists of intra-actions that assemble a 'ghost'. Identity (as an American Civil War soldier) is a particular quality and outcome that emerges out of this relational intra-action. This acknowledges that these 'attached' dead presences and things are themselves the outcome of relationships between them, a past that continues on a present-day battlefield.

The American Civil War battlefield ghost remains an embodiment of a Civil War soldier because its mental processes, which includes the memory of the culture of war and the culture of death, acts and reacts in tandem to imprinted residual rhythms of war that still remains, I propose, embedded on the K.O.C.O.A. of the battlefield. This residual nature of presence 'cues' particular ways that afford reactions on the part of attached presences, based on I.M.P. behaviors and battlefield experience. Such environmental scaffolding affords particular rhythmic behaviors through time that extend out onto the battlefield's K.O.C.O.A. spaces. They 'cue' the memories of those battlefield dead, those not accorded the rite of passage of the Good Death, who still remain (in unmarked graves) on the battlefield.

The 'haunting' assemblage that forms this 'ghost culture' is a grouping of diverse elements, "vibrant materials of all sorts" (Bennett 2010:23). Within this 'haunting' assemblage emerge the 'ghosts', which are always in the process of becoming present. The assemblage is historically (and ethnographically) real. It is not an 'imposition' on the part of the investigator(s), or a perceiving 'witness'.

But any change to an existing embedded network assemblage may result in an entirely new network being produced (Harmon 2009; Fowler and Harris 2015). This is the 'danger' of indiscriminate 'ghost hunting' as scary, but entertaining 'ghost tours' (pop culture entertainment), even changes in habitual rhythms, and historical re-enactments at a location of former (and different) occupational histories, can alter the embedded network assemblage.

This reflects the conditions through which the assemblage of this particular 'ghost culture' is embedded and actualized in particular battlefield K.O.C.O.A. spaces at Burnside Bridge. They reflect sensory spaces that become active in a way that can be experienced as certain kinds of encounters and their remembrances. This affords us to discuss a 'ghost' in a form of presence (a form of life) as a post-human American Civil War soldier. Their documentation becomes a matter of tracing ('excavating') the sensory (and physical non-human) connections across the battlefield's K.O.C.O.A. spaces to reveal particular moments of becoming, when certain situations (performed scenarios) become important.

What this analysis of a 'haunting' assemblage does is to open-up ('unearth') a line of relationality and movement of a 'ghost' becoming present, without resorting to approaches dependent solely on representation (an environmental deviation), idealism (one particular approach based on 'ghost technology'), or skepticism (a mis-interpretation). This is a recognition that there may be different forms of life (as opposed to life forms) and agency in the archaeological record. It recognizes that these different forms have different properties, capacities, affordances, and effects. This includes their agentic roles in assembling and maintain 'haunting' assemblages through time, ones in which we can engage with, in terms of identity.

The temporal continuity of the battlefield's 'sensescape', as a particular attached layer of belief, experience, and memory is thus created by certain emotional acts, including auditory (environmental) soundings, movements, and paths that imprint specific rhythms onto the landscape (in the K.O.C.O.A. spaces). This layer of temporality is a function of "biosocial assemblages" (Ingold and Palsson 2013), interactions between humans and other life forms ('ghosts' and non-humans (environmental elements)), especially prominent in a landscape of 'sacrifice' (violence). This rhythmic interaction becomes a mediation between two worlds and socio-cultural realities.

It is proposed that this type of haunting is based on a culturally-ordered memory. The interpretation of such a haunting must seek to identify the social codes and cultural practices that resulted in the production and retention of this particular sense of place. An inscribed place, such as a battlefield, is not just about physical markers, such as monuments, re-enactments or even graffiti; nor is it about social theater, as in 'living history' practices that 'repeat' the known past. It concerns the social creation, as a communication through time, of memory that produces (and maintains) a particular experience of space. It is one that still haunts the present, principally manifesting today through environmental residual sounds that produce a percolating, ephemeral soundscape of American Civil War combat.

But the right to proper burial, regardless of the significance of the 'home' environment in mid-19th c. America, is a "deeply significant act imbued with meaning" (Parker-Pearson 2003:5). It completes a rite of passage, a cultural intervention that transforms and repositions the dead within society. Death becomes a complex cultural event, a Good Death even more. The American Civil War battlefield changed all that.

In many cases, the social treatment of the battlefield dead did not involve the agency of the living as that cultural rite of passage. The provision for a last resting place for those battlefield dead was not a carefully considered process, in many of these battlefield deaths. This process would have taken time to execute. The result was many hasty burials in mass graves in unknown locations. Some even had no remains to recover and hastily bury, having been obliterated by artillery fire.

Joost Fontein (2010), in his work on Zimbabwean politics of death, argued that attention must be paid to the material aspects of the culturally specific rites and processes of physical transformation "through which the living become properly dead" (2010:437). The "mnemonic technologies of funerals", absent on soldiers missing in battle, negated "the glue that binds rituals and participants together" (Williams 2006:22).

Those mass burials, some still lost on American Civil War battlefields, are not "properly dead". If the location of the dead is an important component in remembering the dead, these unknown locations, besides not being "properly dead", changed the production of a place with which to associate the dead by the living into a 'haunted' place that has produced a legacy that continues to 'haunt' the present, and succeeding generations. The result is that these battlefields have become marked by hauntings, a result of a relational association between unfamiliar, unexpected, violent death, mass burial, and unperformed, still incomplete, rites of passage of the Good Death.

This relational place-marking is an emplacement of an 'afterlife' remembrance. It took place as a need for social recognition, an opposition to loss or exclusion. Such needs imply changes in social circumstances (from peacetime to wartime), and breaks in ritual processes that govern cultural behavior (such as the rite of passage of the Good Death). The concept of liminality is important here. It governs social boundaries, maintains time, rules of conduct, and role expectations. The absence of completion of certain rituals created, I propose, the existence of an (excluded) 'other', the 'battlefield ghost'.

The American Civil War battlefield involved the movements (on an avenue of approach) as a ritual way, a form of 'procession', toward a particular space marked as the 'key area'. The advances (five in all) of Union forces toward Burnside Bridge (the 'key area') was a communal, structured, and directed socio-spatial performance that was the ritualistic act of 'seeing the elephant'.

These acts of advance involved discipline, spatial control, and temporal cadence through a 'liminal' state (the 'obstacle areas') encountered on the way toward the 'key area'. They began with separation in the 'cover and concealed areas'. It ended for many in the liminal space between the 'cover and concealed area' and the 'key area'. Many died without receiving the rite of passage (by surrogates) of the Good Death. It is within these liminal spaces that some dead may remain as embedded 'ghostly presences'. Thus, the K.O.C.O.A. configuration can be viewed as a ritualized landscape of movement and transformation within a theater of war. The ritual of the culture of war either changed the soldier into a survivor of 'seeing the elephant' or, in some cases, created a 'ghostly presence', still in a liminal state of being.

American Civil War combat, as a ritual practice, was a distinctive way of acting and knowing on a battlefield. It included social ('seeing the elephant'), cultural (culture of war/culture of death), spatial (K.O.C.O.A.), temporal (battle), and semiotic (acoustemological) contexts. The ritual was a means (besides victory) to produce a particular social persona, a transformation to a seasoned soldier or veteran.

The consequences of the mass destruction and mass burial of soldiers on these battlefields, without the opportunity for family or surrogate family intervention to complete the rite of passage of the Good Death, moved the consequences far beyond in time from the grief suffered by their relatives. It resulted in multiple affording possibilities of a battlefield becoming embedded with the remains of 'ghost soldiers'. These 'ghost soldiers' became America's first army of the "ghosts of war" (Kwon 2008:15). Today, they represent the "presence and absence of those who have been but are no longer" (Harries 2010:414).

The manifestation of 'ghostly presences' on these American Civil War battlefields serves as a means of affirming the meaning of attachment to a particular place, while simultaneously indicating operating social tensions and conditions that shaped intent and emplacement that created the haunting. This is not just about image, as a pop cultural phenomenon. It is not simply a 'chronotope', a time-space dimension, as ghost stories linked with places. It is not a metaphor for loss (as the 'ghosts of place'), nor is it a mere subjective perception that can be 'debunked' by skeptics.

A haunting with this kind of ghostly presence reinforces a continuity of place and memory. It involves working with a model in which a form of life (a 'ghost') is an actor anchored in (to) time and space, one who is still attached to a particular social (and moral) code. This battlefield haunting is more than "dead memory" (Nora 1989). It exists, as detached ethno-historical knowledge, forming part of the archaeological record of a battlefield taskscape.

These hauntings formed from past productions, emically-centered, in battle where particular acts should have (but in many instances could not have) occurred. A conflict arose between the culture of war and the rite of a 'good death' during this period in history. This conflict created an entangled relationship that became an entrapment of dependence. How could one 'see the elephant', die in the engagement, and still be afforded the rite of passage of the 'good death'? Some, through a 'surrogate family' (fellow soldiers, doctors, nurses, clergy), proxies for those family members who would have surrounded their deathbeds at home, did complete the rite for particular mortally-wounded soldiers before they died. The embodiment of a Good Death via these surrogates was frequently symbolized in the 'condolence letter'. It "represented an initial collaboration between the dying and the living in managing death's terrors" (Faust 2008:144). But many, especially those dying suddenly, did not have that condolence letter written for them.

There was an irreversibility to an entanglement between a battlefield and sudden death. It occurred quite frequently during the American Civil War, and the belief in a 'good death' further entangled the process. The tautness of entanglement further entraps. The advances in new military technology, introduced during the American Civil War, entangled to older Napoleonic military tactics of battle formation and movement led to further entrapment and lessened the possibility of a 'good death', even by a surrogate family member.

The physical destruction of Civil War battle created a societal mess that opened the battlefield space to haunting phenomena. It also changed the presence of present reality from life forms that survived 'seeing the elephant' to an afterlife form of life that remained embedded in layers of memory that remain attached to particular K.O.C.O.A. spaces. Dying, where and how you died, assumed precedence over killing the enemy. The ritual of the 'good death' was shared by all Americans (both North and South), and without regard to religion. There was a great concern for one's own remains after death.

For many who died in battle, especially those who died a 'sudden death', the transformation to, and integration in, a new state of being is still pending. This resulted in a liminal state that is still embedded on the battlefield, and continues to materialize today. It is a wait for the ritual to be completed. The scenarios in which we used investigators as 'surrogate relatives' in search of battlefield MIA, was meant to complete the ritual of the 'good death', and end the liminal state of these 'hauntings'. It was a means to 'unbound' these 'ghosts'. Our entanglement to past social memory, using a "technology of remembrance", suggests a focus on 'how' and 'why' a battlefield haunting could have occurred. It suggests that a mnemonic social 'technology' using a rite of passage may provide the means that binds (and unbounds) the ghosts and investigators together into a relational (and resonating) cultural act of transformation.

In an American Civil War battlefield haunting, geographical space (such as the K.O.C.O.A. configuration), not time (such as the use of 'anniversary dates' by contemporary 'ghost hunters') appears to be significant. It is in these spaces where particular things happened ('seeing the elephant; sudden death), and particular behaviors occurred (The I.M.P. of combat). These 'things' and behaviors were triggered by specific 'soundmarks'. Geography was central, as that place that was not 'home'. That is why our performance practices, both relative to the rite of passage of 'seeing the elephant', and subsequently the rite of passage of the 'good death', related to 'home'.

On these American Civil War battlefields, as continuing 'eventscapes', we still hear the sounds of many deadly stories within still incomplete rites of passage. We can still sense the extent of the horror of the event more than a century later. We feel their presence, we understand their liminal position, and we document their loss. The philosopher Walter <u>Benjamin</u> spoke about *Etngedenken*. This is loosely translated 'remembrance'. It is an act of memory that he defined in terms of a past that will not pass. Is what is still haunting many American Civil War battlefields an example of this 'remembrance'? It is a time that will not pass, a time of liminality because something remains, a presence and ritual awaiting completion.

In this transience and transduction of liminality, the ephemerality of boundaries is breached, as we sense the need and obligation. It creates a shift of position between past and present, absence and presence. We are no longer completely outside the archaeological record, looking at it as strangers. We are inside, looking at something strangely familiar. It is that familiarity that makes a difference, and allows us to care: an archaeology that cares.

The American Civil War battlefield ghost was a witness to, and an ethno-historical explanation of, the 'death' of the 'good death' in mid-19th c. America. To die on a battlefield far from home and family, and without the enactment of a complete ritual of the 'good death', remains, even today, an unresolved issue. The hauntings that are perceived there represent another legacy of the American Civil War. The ghosts become affecting residues of that conflict, reproducing the 'other spatial construct of a battlefield, far from home, family and a 'good death'. It's meaning manifests in multiple senses of loss that have not past. An American Civil War battlefield, in this 'haunting' perspective, is not merely an historical place. It is also a 'sensescape' of a socially- lingering obligation to finally bring those long dead home.

Bibliography

Arensen, Lisa J. 2017. The Dead in the Land: Encounters with Bodies, Bones, and Ghosts in Northwestern Cambodia. *The Journal of Asian Studies.* pp. 1-18.

Armstrong, J. 2010. On the Possibility of a Spectral Ethnography. *Cultural Studies/Critical Methodologies* 10(3):243-50.

Barrett, John. 1991. Towards an Archaeology of Ritual in *Sacred and Profane: Proceedings of a Conference on Archaeology, Ritual, and Religion.* Oxford 1989. Edited by Paul Garwood, David Jennings, Robin Skeates, and Judith Toms. Oxford University Committee for Archaeology Monograph No. 32. pp. 1-9.

1994. *Fragments From Antiquity: An Archaeology of Social Life in Britain 2900-1200 B.C.* Oxford: Blackwell.

Barth, F. 1987. *Cosmologies in the Making: A Generative Approach to Cultural Variation in Inner New Guinea.* Cambridge: Cambridge University Press.

Bennett, Jane. 2010. *Vibrant Matter: A Political Ecology of Things.* Duke University Press.

Bird-David, Nurit. 1999. Animinism Revisited: Personhood, Environment, and Relational Epistemology. *Current Anthropology* 40:S67-S91.

Blanco, Maria del Pilar and Ester Pereen (Editors). 2010. *Popular Ghosts: The Haunted Spaces of Everyday Culture.* New York: The Continuum International Publishing Group, Inc.

Blanco, Maria del Pilar and Ester Peeren. 2013. *The Spectralities Reader: Ghosts and Haunting in Contemporary Cultural Theory.* London: Bloomsburg.

Blauner, Robert. 1966. Death and Social Strtucture. *Psychiatry* 29:378-394.

Bloch, M. 1977. The Past and the Present in the Present. *MAN 12:* 278-292.

Budrewicz, Z., Sendyka, R. and Nycz R. (Editors). 2014. *Pamiec I Afekty.* Warszawa: Instytut Badan Literackich PAN.

Cameron, E. Indigenous Spectrality and the Politics of Postcolonial Ghost Stories. *Cultural Geographies* 15(3): 383-393.

Cannadine, David. 1983. The Context, Performance, and Meaning of Ritual: The British Monarchy and the "Invention of Tradition" in *The Invention of Tradition.* Edited by Eric Hobsdbawn and Terrance

Ranger. Cambridge: Cambridge University Press. pp. 101-164.

Carlson, Marvin. 1996. *Performance: A Critical Introduction.* London: Routledge.

Carman, John. 1999. *Ancient Warfare: Archaeological Perspectives.* Stroud, Gloucestershire: Sutton Pub.

Clarke, Roger. 2013. *A Natural History of Ghosts: 500 Years of Hunting for Proof.* Penguin Books.

Detzer, David. 2004. *Donnybrook: The Battle of Bull Run, 1861.* New York: Harcourt, Inc.

Dwyer, O.J. and Alderman, Derek H. 2008. Memorial Landscapes: Analytic Questions and Metaphors. *Geo. Journal* 73:165-178.

Espenshade, Christopher T., Robert L. Jolley, and James B. Legg. 2002. The Value and Treatment of Civil War Military Sites. *North*

American Archaeologist Volume 23(1): 39-67.

Faust, Drew Gilpin. 2008. *This Republic of Suffering: Death and the American Civil War.* New York: Alfred a. Knopf.

Favret-Saada, Jeanne. 1980. *Deadly Words: Witchcraft in the Bocage.* Cambridge: Cambridge University Press.

Feld, Steven. 1994. Communication, Music, and Speech in Steven Feld and Charis Keil (Editors) *About Music: Music Grooves.* Chicago: University of Chicago Press. pp. 77-95.

1996. Waterfalls of Song: An Acoustemology of Place Resounding in Bosavi, Papua New Guinea in *Senses of Place.* Edited by Steven Feld and Keith H. Basso. Santa Fe: School of American Research Press. pp. 91-136.

Ferrell, J. 2015. Ghost Ethnography: On Crimes Against Reality. Paper presented at

Crimes Against Reality University of Hamburg, Germany.

Fontein, Joost. 2010. Between Tortured Bodies and Resurfacing Bones: The Politics of the Dead in Zimbabwe. *Journal of Material Culture* 15(4):423-48.

Fowler, C. and O.J.T. Harris. 2015. Enduring Relations: Exploring a Paradox of New Materialism. *Journal of Material Culture* 20(2): 127-148).

Fox, James. 1973. On Bad Death and the Left Hand: A Study of Rotinese Symbolic Inversions in *Right and Left: Essays on Dual Symbolic Classification.* Edited by R. Needham. Chicago: University of Chicago Press.

Gheorghiu, Dragos and George Nash (Editors). 2013. *Place as Material Culture: Objects, Geographies, and the Construction of Time.* Newcastle upon Tyne, U.K: Cambridge Scholars Publishers.

Gibson, J. *The Ecological Approach to Visual Perception.* Hillsdale, New Jersey: Lawrence Eribaum.

Gunning, Tom. 2008. Reflections, Modern Illusion: Sighting the Modern Optical Uncanny in J. Collis and J. Jervis (Editors) *Uncanny Modernity: Cultural Theories, Modern Anxieties.* Houndmills, Basingstoke, and Harts: Palgrave Macmillan. Pp. 68-90.

Gustafsson, Mai Lan. 2009. *War and Shadows: The Haunting of Vietnam.* Ithaca: Cornell University Press.

Haraway, Donna. 1988. Situated Knowledges: The Science Question in *Feminist Studies* 14(3):575-599.

Harjumaa, P. 2008. Aaveriekkoja: Lappilaisia Mystisia Tarinoita ja Kummituksia. Rovaniemi: Lapland University Press.

Harmon, G. 2009. *Prince of Networks: Bruno Latour and Metaphysics.* Melbourne: Re. Press.

Harries, John. 2010. Of Bleeding Skulls and the PostColonial Uncanny: Bones and the presence of Nonosabasut and Demasduit. *Journal of Material Culture* 15(4):403-421.

Harrison, Rodney. 2011. Surface Assemblages: Toward an Archaeology *In* and *of* the Present. *Archaeological Dialogues* 18(2):141-161.

Hayward, K. 2012. Five Spaces of Cultural Criminology. *British Journal of Criminology* 52(3):441-462.

Herva, Vesa-Pekka. 2014. Haunted Heritage in an Enchanted Land: Magic, Materiality, and Second World War German Material Heritage in Finnish Lapland. *Journal of Contemporary Archaeology* 1.2: 297-321.

Hodder, Ian. 1978. Social Organization and Human Interaction: The Development of Some Tentative Hypotheses in *Terms of Material Culture in the Spatial Organization of Culture.* London: Duckworth. pp. 190-270.

2012. *Entangled: An Archaeology of the Relationships Between Humans and Things.* Oxford: Wiley-Blackwell.

Holloway, J.   Legend-Tripping in Spooky Spaces: Ghost Tourism and Infrastructures of Enchantment. *Environment and Planning D* 28: 618-637.

Holtorf, Cornelius. 2005. *From Stonehenge to Las Vegas: Archaeology as Popular Culture.* Walnut Creek, California: AltaMira Press.

Hudson, Martyn. 2017. *Ghosts, Landscapes and Social Memory.* New York: Routledge.

Ingold, Tim and J. Verqunst (Editors). 2008. Introduction in *Ways of Walking:*

Ethnography and Practice on Foot. Aldershot: Ashgate. pp. 1-20.

2011. *Redrawing Anthropology: Materials, Movements, Lines.* Ashgate, Aldershot.

Ingodd, T. and Palsson, Gisli. 2013. *Biosocial Becomings: Integrating Social and Biological Anthropology.* Cambridge: Cambridge University Press.

Inwood, J. 2009. Searching for the Promised Land: Examining Dr. Martin Luther King's Concept of the Beloved Community. *Antipode* 41:487-508.

Jorge, Vitor Oliveira. 2007. Archaeological Excavation as Performance: Dissolving Boundaries Between Art and Science for the Sake of Knowledge. T.A.G. 2007. Dept. of Archaeology, University of York. December 14-16.

Keegan, John. 1993. *A History of Warfare.* Random House.

Keeley, L.H. 1996. *War Before Civilization.* Oxford: Oxford University Press.

Kerns, S. 1983. *The Culture of Time and Space, 1880-1918.* Cambridge: Blackwell.

Kristiansen, K. 2011. Constructing Social and Cultural Identity in the Bronze Age in Robert, B.W. and M. Vander Linden (Editors). *Investigating Archaeological Cultures: Material Culture, Variability, and Transmission.* London: Springer.

Kwon, Heonik. 2006. *After the Massacre: Commemoration and Consolation in Ha My and My Lai.* Berkeley: University of California Press.

2008. *Ghosts of War in Vietnam.* Cambridge: Cambridge University Press.

Ladwig, Patrice. 2012. Can Things Reach the Dead? The Ontological Status of Objects and the Study of Lao Buddhist Rituals for the Spirits of the Deceased in Edres, Kirsten and

Andrea Lauser (Editors). *Engaging the Spirit World in Modern SE Asia.* New York: Oxford Berghahn.

Lambek, Michael. 1981. *Human Spirits: A Cultural Account of Trance in Mayotte.* Cambridge: Cambridge University Press.

Lee, Christina (Editor). 2017. *Spectral Spaces and Hauntings: The Affects of Absence.* New York: Routledge.

Leeder, Murray. 2014. Victorian Science and Spiritualism in the Legend of Hell House. *Horror Studies* 5(1):31-46.

Lesser, Alexander. 1961. Social Fields and the Evolution of Society. *Southwestern Journal of Anthropology* 18: 40-48.

Lipman, Caron. 2014. *Co-habiting with Ghosts: Knowledge, Experience, Belief, and the Domestic Uncanny.* New York: Routledge.

Lloyd, D.W. 1994. Tourism, Pilgrimage, and the Commemoration of the Great War in Great Britain, Australia, and Canada 1919-1939. PhD Thesis: Cambridge University.

Malarney, Shaun Kingsley. 2001. The Fatherland Remembers Your Sacrifice: Commemorating War Dead in North Vietnam in *The Country of Memory: Remaking the Past in Late Socialist Vietnam.* Edited by H.T.H. Tai. Berkeley: University of California press. pp. 46-76.

2002. *Culture, Ritual, and Revolution in Vietnam.* New York: Routledge.

McLuhan, Marshall. `1969. *The Medium is the Message.* New York: Bantam.

Metcalf, Peter. 2001. Global Disjuncture and the 'Sites' of Anthropology. *Cultural Anthropology* 16(2): 165-82.

Middleton, John. 1982. Lugbara Death in M. Bloch and J. Parry (Editors) *Death and the*

Regeneration of Life. Cambridge: Cambridge University Press.

Mitchell, Reid. 2000. *The Vacant Chair: The Northern Soldier Leaves Home.* New York: Oxford University Press.

Navaro, Yael. 2012. *The Make-Believe Space: Affective Geography in a Postwar Polity.* Durham: Duke University Press.

Nora, Pierre. 1989. Memory and History. *Representations.* No. 26: 7-24.

Orr, David G. 1994. The Archaeology of Trauma: An Introduction to the Historical Archaeology of the American Civil War in *Look to the Earth: Historical Archaeology and the American Civil War.* Edited by Charles R. Geier and Susan E. Winter. Knoxville: University of Tennessee Press. pp. 21-35.

Pauketat, Timothy. 2001. Practice and History in Archaeology: An Emerging

Paradigm. *Anthropological Theory* 1(1):73-98.

Pearson, Mike and Michael Shanks. 2001. *Theatre/Archaeology.* London: Routledge.

Preucel, Robert. 2016. Pragmatic Archaeology and Semiotic Mediation. *Semiotic Review* November 14: 1-8.

Rainey, Rueben M. 1997. Hallowed Grounds and Rituals of Remembrance: Union Regimental Monuments at Gettysburg in *Understanding Ordinary Landscapes.* Edited by Paul Groth and Todd W. Bressi. New Haven: Yale University Press. pp. 67-80.

Richards, C. and Thomas, J. 1984. Ritual Activity and Structured Deposition in Late Neolithic Wessex in R. Bradley and J. Gardiner (Editors) *Neolithic Studies: A Review of Some Current Research.* Oxford. Pp. 189-218.

Roberts, Nancy. 1992. *Civil War Ghost Stories and Legends.* Columbia, South Carolina: University of South Carolina Press.

Rowlands, Mark. 2010. *The New Science of the Mind: From Extended Mind to Embodied Phenomenology.* London: MIT Press.

Sabol, John G. 2007. *Battlefield Hauntscape: The Unearthing of Gettysburg, July 1863.* Bloomington, Indiana: AuthorHouse.

2013. *Burnside Bridge.* Brunswick, Maryland: Ghost Excavation Books, Inc.

2014a. *The Good Death and the Civil War: The Haunting of an American Battlefield.* Bedford, Pennsylvania: Ghost Excavation Books, Inc.

2014b. *Archaeology and Ghost Research: A Relational Entanglement.* Bedford, Pennsylvania: Ghost Excavation Books, Inc.

2015. *Haunting Presences, Ruins, and Ghostly Entanglements: Excavations at the Edge of Performance.* Bedford, Pennsylvania: Ghost Excavation Books, Inc.

Schafer, Murray R. 1977. *The Soundscape: The Tuning of the World.* New York: Alfred A. Knopf.

Sexton, J. Weird Britain in Exile: Ghost Box, Hauntology, and Alternative Heritage. *Popular Music and Society 35(4): 561-584.*

Skinner, Ryan, 2005. Unpublished Paper: The Social Science of Audition. Academia.edu.

Stewart, S. 1994. *On Longing: Narratives of the Miniature, the Gigantic, the Souvenir, the Collection.* Durham, North Carolina: Duke University Press.

Tedlock, Denis. 1991. From Participant Observation to the Observation of Participation: The Emergence of Narrative.

Ethnographic Journal of Anthropological Research 47(1): 69-94.

Thorn, Raimond. 2013. The Importance of Acoustics and Illumination When Creating a Chronotope: Reflections About Two Middle Neolithic Palisades From Southern Sweden. pp. 123-133 in *Place as Material Culture: Objects, Geographies, and the Construction of Time.* Edited by Dragos Gheorghiu and George Nash Newcastle upon Tyne, U.K: Cambridge Scholars Publishers.

Tilley, C. 1989. Excavation as Theatre. *Antiquity* 63 (239): 275-280.

1994. *A Phenomenology of Landscape: Places, Paths, and Monuments.* Bloomsbury Academic

Tuan, Y. F. 1977. *Space and Place: The Perspective of Experience.* Minneapolis: University of Minnesota Press.

Van Gennep, Arnold. 1960. *The Rites of Passage.* Chicago: University of Chicago Press.

Williams, H. 2006. *Death and Memory in Early Medieval Britain.* Cambridge: Cambridge University Press.

Winter, J. 1995. *Death's Men: Soldiers of the Great War.* Harmonsworth: Penguin.

Vannini, P. 2015. Non-Representational Ethnography: New Ways of Animating Lifeworlds. *Cultural Geographies* 22(2):317-327.

About the Author

Photo 14: The Author

John Sabol is an archaeologist, cultural anthropologist, actor, and author. As an archaeologist, he has unearthed past material remains in excavations and site surveys in England, Mexico, and at various sites in the United States (including Eastern South Dakota, the Tennessee River Valleys, and in Pennsylvania). His anthropological fieldwork includes the studies of "spirits" in the religious beliefs of the afterlife among various cultural groups in Mexico (Mixtec, Zapotec, Lacandon, Nahuatl, and Otomi). His acting career includes "ghosting" performances of various characters and scenarios in more than 35 movies, TV shows, and documentaries. He has appeared in the A&E TV series, Paranormal State as an investigative consultant. He has written over thirty books.

His recent speaking engagements include the T.A.G. (Theoretical Archaeology Group) Conference at the University of California, Berkeley, at the Space and Place Conference in Prague, Czech Republic, the TAG Conference at the University in Buffalo, New York, Exploring the Extraordinary Conference in York, England, the C.H.A.T. archaeological conference also in York, and the GHost Conference at the University of London, London, England.

His investigative reports have been published in such diverse venues as Haunted Times Magazine, Tennessee Anthropologist, and the online journal, ParaAnthropology. He has been a frequent guest on numerous radio and internet talk shows, among them, Beyond the Edge Radio, The Paranormal View, Para X Radio, Blog Talk Radio, The Grand Dark Conspiracy, and Rusty O'Nhiall's "Mysterious and Unexplained" on PsiFM (Australia). He was a university professor in Mexico for 11 years, teaching both undergraduate and graduate courses on the anthropology of tourism. He has also been featured on public educational TV for U.S. and foreign markets, and has worked on international educational documentaries (in Spain).

He has a M.A. in Anthropology/Archaeology (University of Tennessee), and a B.A. in Sociology/Anthropology (Bloomsburg University). He has also attended Penn State University, the University of Pittsburgh, the University of the Americas (Cholula, Puebla, Mexico), and has studied theatre and method acting in Mexico City.

Websites

www.ghostexcavation.com

www.imdb.com/name/nm1254777/

utk.academia.edu/JohnSabol

www.ingramcontent.com/pod-product-compliance
Lightning Source LLC
Chambersburg PA
CBHW050824260726
48660CB00004B/1589